The Ultimate Halal Cookbook

Amazing Halal Recipes You Can Make at Home!!

Table of Contents

Introduction

This Halal cookbook contains recipes from all over the world. You'll learn different halal recipes from all over the globe. These recipes are collections of culinary customs and delicious entrees filled with diverse flavors.

All recipes in the book contain recipes with only halal ingredients. So, you don't have to worry about accidentally making a non-halal meal. These delicious halal recipes are perfect to share with family and friends. If you've got a passion for halal cooking and are ready to take your cooking up a notch turn the page.

Main Course

Recipe 1. Shawarma

Serves: 2

Preparation Time: 10 minutes

Cooking Time: 10 minutes

The List of Ingredients:

1. 2-3 green chilies, finely chopped
2. 1 cup halal mayonnaise
3. 2 large bread
4. Salt and pepper to taste

5. A handful of fresh coriander leaves

6. 1/2 pound roasted halal chicken, minced

Method:

Step 1   Combine all the ingredients in a large bowl. Mix
          well and keep aside.

Step 2   Heat each side of both flatbreads in a non-stick
          pan over medium-high until golden.

Step 3   Now place a flatbread over the chopping board
          and put 1/2 of the prepared mix on the edge.
          Then roll the flatbread towards the other edge.

Step 4   Repeat the same method and make another
          shawarma.

Step 5   Serve hot!

Recipe 2. Tandoori Turkey

Serves: 2

Preparation Time: 10 minutes

Cooking Time: 30 minutes

The List of Ingredients:

1. 2-3 cardamoms, ground
2. A handful of fresh coriander leaves
3. 1/4 teaspoon chili powder
4. 1 pound halal turkey breast, boneless and diced

5. 1 teaspoon freshly grated garlic

6. 1 teaspoon freshly grated ginger

7. 1 cup yogurt

8. 1/2 cup mustard oil

9. Salt to taste

Method:

Step 1   Combine all the ingredients in a large bowl and mix well with hand until turkey chunks are evenly coated with the mixture.

Step 2   Then, cover the bowl with a cling wrap and refrigerate for 4-5 hours.

Step 3   Heat mustard oil in a deep and large non-stick pan over medium-high heat. Take out the bowl from the refrigerator and put the marinated turkey pieces in the pan. Cook until turkey pieces are cooked through.

Step 4   Once done, remove the pan from heat and transfer the turkey to a serving platter.

Step 5   Serve hot with mint sauce.

Recipe 3. Chana Mutton

Serves: 2

Preparation Time: 10 minutes

Cooking Time: 30 minutes

The List of Ingredients:

1. 2-3 cardamoms, ground
2. 1/2 pound butter-fried halal goat, diced
3. A handful of fresh coriander leaves
4. 2 cups freshly pureed tomatoes

5. 1/2 cup butter

6. 1 teaspoon freshly grated garlic

7. 1 large onion, finely chopped

8. Salt and pepper to taste

9. 2 cups boiled split chickpeas

10. A dash of cinnamon

11. 1 teaspoon freshly grated ginger

12. 2-3 cloves, crushed

Method:

Step 1   Melt butter in a deep and large non-stick pan over medium-high heat. Stir in onion and sauté until translucent. Add in ginger and garlic. Cook for a few minutes.

Step 2   Then, add in tomatoes and cook until everything turns into a thick gravy.

Step 3   Now, add in the rest of the ingredients. Cover the pan with a lid and let it simmer over low for 15-20, stirring occasionally.

Step 4   Once done, remove the pan from heat and transfer the dish to a serving bowl.

Step 5   Serve hot with naan bread.

Recipe 4. Shami Kebabs

Servings: 8

Preparation Time: 20 minutes

Cooking Time: 45 minutes

The List of Ingredients:

1. 1/2 pound butter-fried halal goat, minced
2. 1 teaspoon freshly grated garlic
3. 1 large onion, finely chopped
4. A handful of mint leaves

5. 2-3 cloves, crushed

6. 2-3 cardamoms, ground

7. 4 tablespoons olive oil

8. Salt and pepper to taste

9. 1 teaspoon freshly grated ginger

10. A handful of fresh coriander leaves

11. 2 tablespoons butter

12. A dash of cinnamon

Method:

Step 1   Melt butter in a deep and large non-stick pan over medium-high heat. Stir in onion and sauté until translucent. Add in ginger and garlic. Cook for a few minutes.

Step 2   Now, add in the rest of the ingredients. Cook over low for 15-20, stirring occasionally.

Step 3   Once done, remove the pan from heat and let it cool down.

Step 4   Once cool, blend the mixture in a food processor until smooth.

Step 5   Then, transfer the mix to a bowl and cover it with a cling wrap. Refrigerate for 3-4 hours.

Step 6   Take out the bowl from the refrigerator and make 8 flat patties and keep aside.

Step 7   Heat olive oil in a leg non-stick pan over medium-high flame. Shallow fry both sides of prepared kebabs until golden brown.

Step 8   Serve hot with chutney!

Recipe 5. Salmon Curry

Serves: 2

Preparation Time: 10 minutes

Cooking Time: 30 minutes

The List of Ingredients:

1. A handful of fresh coriander leaves

2. 2 teaspoons dried coriander powder

3. 1 teaspoon freshly grated ginger

4. 1 large onion, finely chopped

5. 1/2 quart water

6. 1/2 pound halal salmon, diced

7. 1 teaspoon freshly grated garlic

8. 1/2 cup butter

9. Salt and pepper to taste

10. 2 cups freshly pureed tomatoes

Method:

Step 1   Melt butter in a deep and large non-stick pan over medium-high heat. Stir in onion and sauté until translucent. Add in ginger and garlic. Cook for a few minutes.

Step 2   Then, add in tomatoes and cook until everything turns into a thick gravy.

Step 3   Now, add in the rest of the ingredients. Cover the pan with a lid and let it simmer over low for 15-20, stirring occasionally.

Step 4   Once done, remove the pan from heat and transfer the dish to a serving bowl.

Step 5   Serve hot with boiled rice.

Recipe 6. Butter Chicken

Serves: 2

Preparation Time: 10 minutes

Cooking Time: 30 minutes

The List of Ingredients:

1. 1 large onion, finely chopped

2. A handful of cashews, blended

3. 1 teaspoon freshly grated ginger

4. 2 cups freshly pureed tomatoes

5. 1/2 cup low-fat heavy cream

6. Salt and pepper to taste

7. 2 tablespoons butter

8. 2-3 cardamoms, ground

9. 1/2 pound roasted halal chicken breast, diced (boneless and skinless)

10. 1 teaspoon freshly grated garlic

11. 1 tablespoon dried fenugreek leaves

Method:

Step 1 Melt butter in a deep and large non-stick pan over medium-high heat. Stir in onion and sauté until translucent. Add in ginger and garlic. Cook for a few minutes.

Step 2 Then, add in tomatoes and cook until everything turns into a thick gravy.

Step 3 Once done, remove the pan from heat and let it cool down till it comes to room temperature.

Step 4 Once cool, blend the prepared mix in a food processor until smooth.

Step 5 Now, pour the mix back into the pan and add in the rest of the ingredients. Cover the pan with a lid and let it simmer over low for 15-20, stirring occasionally.

Step 6   Once done, remove the pan from heat and transfer the chicken to a serving bowl.

Step 7   Serve hot with naan bread or rice.

Recipe 7. Haleem

Serves: 2

Preparation Time: 10 minutes

Cooking Time: 30 minutes

The List of Ingredients:

1. 1 teaspoon freshly grated garlic
2. 1 teaspoon freshly grated ginger
3. 2 cups boiled split chickpeas

4. 2-3 cardamoms, ground

5. 1 large onion, finely chopped

6. A dash of cinnamon

7. 1/2 pound butter-fried halal beef, minced

8. 2-3 cloves, crushed

9. 1/2 cup butter

10. 2 cups freshly pureed tomatoes

11. A handful of fresh coriander leaves

12. Salt and pepper to taste

Method:

Step 1   Blend minced and split chickpeas along with 2 cups of water in a food processor until smooth. Keep aside.

Step 2   Melt butter in a deep and large non-stick pan over medium-high heat. Stir in onion and sauté until translucent. Add in ginger and garlic. Cook for a few minutes.

Step 3   Then, add in tomatoes and cook until everything turns into a thick gravy.

Step 4   Now, add in the rest of the ingredients and blended mix. Cover the pan with a lid and let it simmer over low for 15-20, stirring occasionally.

Step 5   Once done, remove the pan from heat and transfer the dish to a serving bowl.

Step 6   Serve hot with naan bread or rice.

Recipe 8. Potato Bharta

Serves: 2

Preparation Time: 10 minutes

Cooking Time: 30 minutes

The List of Ingredients:

1. A handful of fresh coriander leaves
2. 1 large onion, finely chopped
3. 1 teaspoon freshly grated ginger
4. 1 teaspoon freshly grated garlic

5. 2 medium potatoes, peeled and mashed

6. 2 cups freshly pureed tomatoes

7. 1/2 cup butter

8. Salt and pepper to taste

9. 1 cup green pea kernels

Method:

Step 1   Melt butter in a deep and large non-stick pan over medium-high heat. Stir in onion and sauté until translucent. Add in ginger and garlic. Cook for a few minutes.

Step 2   Then, add in tomatoes and cook until everything turns into a thick gravy.

Step 3   Now, add in the rest of the ingredients. Cover the pan with a lid and let it simmer over low for 15-20, stirring occasionally.

Step 4   Once done, remove the pan from heat and transfer the dish to a serving bowl.

Step 5   Serve hot with naan bread.

Recipe 9. Dahi Murg

Serves: 2

Preparation Time: 10 minutes

Cooking Time: 30 minutes

The List of Ingredients:

1. 1 cup sour cream

2. Salt and pepper to taste

3. 2 cups boiled split chickpeas

4. 1/2 pound halal chicken drumsticks

5. A handful of fresh coriander leaves

6. 1 spring onion, finely chopped

7. 1 teaspoon freshly grated ginger

8. 1/2 cup butter

9. 2 cups yogurt

10. 1 teaspoon freshly grated garlic

11. 2-3 cardamoms, ground

Method:

Step 1   Melt butter in a deep and large non-stick pan over medium-high heat. Add in ginger and garlic. Cook for a few minutes.

Step 2   Now, add in the rest of the ingredients. Cover the pan with a lid and let it simmer over low heat until chicken is cooked through, stirring occasionally.

Step 3   Once done, remove the pan from heat and transfer the dish to a serving bowl.

Step 4   Serve hot with naan bread.

Recipe 10. Roghan Josh

Serves: 2

Preparation Time: 10 minutes

Cooking Time: 30 minutes

The List of Ingredients:

1. 2-3 cardamoms, ground
2. 1 teaspoon freshly grated ginger
3. 1 large onion, finely chopped
4. A dash of cinnamon

5. A handful of fresh coriander leaves

6. 2 cups freshly pureed tomatoes

7. Salt and pepper to taste

8. 1 teaspoon freshly grated garlic

9. 1/2 cup butter

10. 2-3 cloves, crushed

11. 1/2 pound butter-fried halal goat, diced

Method:

Step 1 Melt butter in a deep and large non-stick pan over medium-high heat. Stir in onion and sauté until translucent. Add in ginger and garlic. Cook for a few minutes.

Step 2 Then, add in tomatoes and cook until everything turns into a thick gravy.

Step 3 Now, add in the rest of the ingredients. Cover the pan with a lid and let it simmer over low for 15-20, stirring occasionally.

Step 4 Once done, remove the pan from heat and transfer the dish to a serving bowl.

Step 5 Serve hot with naan bread.

Recipe 11. Carrot Green Pea Pulao

Serves: 2

Preparation Time: 10 minutes

Cooking Time: 30 minutes

The List of Ingredients:

1. 2 tablespoons butter
2. 4 cups water
3. 1 teaspoon freshly grated garlic
4. Salt and pepper to taste

5. 2 cups basmati rice

6. 2 cups carrot, chopped

7. 1 teaspoon cumin seeds

8. 1 teaspoon freshly grated ginger

9. 1 cup green pea kernels

10. 1 large onion, finely chopped

Method:

Step 1 Melt butter in a deep and large non-stick pan over medium-high heat. Add in cumin seeds and cook until golden. Stir in onion and sauté until translucent. Add in ginger and garlic. Cook for a few minutes.

Step 2 Now, add in the rest of the ingredients. Cover the pan with a lid and let it simmer over low heat until water evaporates completely and rice is cooked through, stirring occasionally.

Step 3 Once done, remove the pan from heat and transfer the pulao to a serving bowl.

Step 4 Serve hot with naan bread.

Recipe 12. Beef Ball Corn Curry

Serves: 2

Preparation Time: 10 minutes

Cooking Time: 30 minutes

The List of Ingredients:

1. Fresh coriander leaves (handful)

2. Pepper and salt to taste

3. 8 small halal beef balls

4. 1 large onion, chopped finely

5. 1 teaspoon freshly grated garlic

6. 2 cups freshly pureed tomatoes

7. 2 cups corn kernels

8. 1/2 cup butter

9. 1 teaspoon freshly grated ginger

10. 1/2 quart water

Method:

Step 1   Melt butter in a deep and large non-stick pan over medium-high heat. Stir in onion and sauté until translucent. Add in ginger and garlic. Cook for a few minutes.

Step 2   Then, add in tomatoes and cook until everything turns into a thick gravy.

Step 3   Now, add in the rest of the ingredients except beef balls. Cover the pan with a lid and let it simmer over low for 15-20, stirring occasionally.

Step 4   Once done, add in beef balls and cook for a minute.

Step 5   Then, remove the pan from heat and transfer the dish to a serving bowl.

Step 6   Serve hot with rice.

Recipe 13. Beef Biryani

Serves: 2

Preparation Time: 10 minutes

Cooking Time: 30 minutes

The List of Ingredients:

1. A dash of cinnamon

2. 1 tablespoon black peppercorns

3. A handful of roasted cashews

4. 1 large onion, thinly sliced

5. 1 teaspoon freshly grated garlic

6. 1 teaspoon freshly grated ginger

7. 6 cups boiled rice

8. 1/2 pound butter-fried beef, diced

9. Few strings of saffron soaked in 1/4 cup milk

10. 4 tablespoons butter

11. Salt to taste

12. 2-3 cloves

13. 2-3 cardamoms, crushed

Method:

Step 1   Melt butter in a deep and large non-stick pan over medium-high heat. Stir in onion and sauté until translucent. Add in ginger and garlic. Cook for a few minutes.

Step 2   Then, add in the rest of the ingredients. Cover the pan with a lid and let it simmer over low for 15-20, stirring occasionally.

Step 3   Once done, remove the pan from heat and transfer the biryani to a serving bowl.

Step 4   Serve hot.

Recipe 14. Egg Cauliflower Sabzi

Serves: 2

Preparation Time: 10 minutes

Cooking Time: 30 minutes

The List of Ingredients:

1. Salt and pepper to taste
2. 1 small head of cauliflower head, grated
3. 1 teaspoon freshly grated garlic
4. 2 tablespoon olive oil

5. 2 cups freshly pureed tomatoes

6. A handful of fresh coriander leaves

7. 1 large onion, finely chopped

8. 2 cups water

9. 1 teaspoon freshly grated ginger

10. 2 hardboiled eggs, grated

Method:

Step 1   Heat oil in a deep and large non-stick pan over medium-high flame. Stir in onion and sauté until translucent. Add in ginger and garlic. Cook for a few minutes.

Step 2   Then, add in tomatoes and cook until everything turns into a thick gravy.

Step 3   Now, add in the rest of the ingredients. Cover the pan with a lid and let it simmer over low until water evaporates completely, stirring occasionally.

Step 4   Once done, remove the pan from heat and transfer the dish to a serving bowl.

Step 5   Serve hot with naan bread.

Soups

Recipe 15. Broccoli Rice Soup

Serves: 2

Preparation Time: 10 minutes

Cooking Time: 30 minutes

The List of Ingredients:

1. 2 tablespoons butter
2. Salt and pepper as desired
3. Florets of 1 small head of broccoli
4. 1 cup rice, rinsed

5. 1 quart vegetable stock

6. 1 tablespoon oregano

Method:

Step 1   Put all ingredients in a deep-bottom pan.

Step 2   Use a lid to cover the pan. Let it simmer over the low heat until ingredients are cooked through and water reduces to half.

Step 3   Once ready, remove the pan from the heat and pour the soup into 2 bowls.

Step 4   Serve hot!

Recipe 16. Bell Pepper Beef Soup

Serves: 2

Preparation Time: 10 minutes

Cooking Time: 30 minutes

The List of Ingredients:

1. 1/2 pound butter-fried halal minced beef

2. 1 quart halal chicken stock

3. 1 large green bell pepper, chopped

4. A dash of cinnamon

5. 2 tablespoons butter

6. Salt and pepper to taste

Method:

Step 1   Put all the ingredients in a deep bottom pan.

Step 2   Cover the pan with a lid. Let it simmer over low heat until ingredients are cooked through and water reduces to half.

Step 3   Once ready, remove the pan from heat and pour the soup into 2 bowls.

Step 4   Serve hot!

Recipe 17. Carrot Scallop Soup

Serves: 2

Preparation Time: 10 minutes

Cooking Time: 30 minutes

The List of Ingredients:

1. 1/4 pound carrots, chopped
2. Salt and pepper to taste
3. 1 tablespoon chives, chopped
4. 1 quart halal chicken stock

5. 2 tablespoons butter

6. 1/4 pound halal scallops

Method:

Step 1   Put all the ingredients in a deep bottom pan.

Step 2   Cover the pan with a lid. Let it simmer over low heat until ingredients are cooked through and water reduces to half.

Step 3   Once ready, remove the pan from heat and pour the soup into 2 bowls.

Step 4   Serve hot!

Recipe 18. Salmon Jalapeno Soup

Serves: 2

Preparation Time: 10 minutes

Cooking Time: 30 minutes

The List of Ingredients:

1. 2 tablespoons butter
2. 1 quart halal chicken stock
3. Salt and pepper to taste
4. 1/2 pound halal salmon, diced

5. 1 tablespoon oregano

6. 1 cup fresh jalapeño, chopped

Method:

Step 1   Put all the ingredients in a deep bottom pan.

Step 2   Cover the pan with a lid. Let it simmer over low heat until ingredients are cooked through and water reduces to half.

Step 3   Once ready, remove the pan from heat and pour the soup into 2 bowls.

Step 4   Serve hot!

Recipe 19. Corn Garlic Soup

Serves: 2

Preparation Time: 10 minutes

Cooking Time: 30 minutes

The List of Ingredients:

1. 4 cups sweet corn kernels
2. 2 tablespoons butter
3. 2 tablespoons freshly grated garlic
4. Salt and pepper as desired

5. 1 quart vegetable stock

6. 2-3 spring onions, chopped

Method:

Step 1   Put all ingredients in a deep-bottom pan.

Step 2   Use a lid to cover the pan. Let it simmer over the low heat until water reduces to half.

Step 3   Once ready, remove the pan from the heat and pour the soup into 2 bowls.

Step 4   Serve hot!

Recipe 20. Ginger Potato Soup

Serves: 2

Preparation Time: 10 minutes

Cooking Time: 30 minutes

The List of Ingredients:

1. 1 tablespoon fresh lemongrass, chopped
2. 1 quart vegetable stock
3. 2 medium potatoes, chopped
4. Salt and pepper to taste

5. 2 tablespoons butter

6. 2 tablespoons freshly grated ginger

Method:

Step 1   Put all the ingredients in a deep bottom pan.

Step 2   Cover the pan with a lid. Let it simmer over low
          heat until ingredients are cooked through and
          water reduces to half.

Step 3   Once ready, remove the pan from heat and pour
          the soup into 2 bowls.

Step 4   Serve hot!

Recipe 21. Murg Clove Shorba

Serves: 2

Preparation Time: 10 minutes

Cooking Time: 30 minutes

The List of Ingredients:

1. 1 quart halal chicken stock
2. 1 cup coconut milk
3. 1/2 pound halal chicken breast, boneless
4. 2 tablespoons butter

  5. 2-3 cloves, crushed

  6. Salt and pepper to taste

Method:

Step 1   Put all the ingredients in a deep bottom pan.

Step 2   Cover the pan with a lid. Let it simmer over low heat until chicken is cooked through and water reduces to half.

Step 3   Once cooked, remove the lid and take out a chicken breast from the soup. Shred the chicken with a fork and put it back in the pan with soup. Cook for another 5 minutes over high heat, stirring occasionally.

Step 4   Once ready, remove the pan from heat and pour the soup into 2 bowls.

Step 5   Serve hot!

Recipe 22. Spring Onion Egg Soup

Serves: 2

Preparation Time: 10 minutes

Cooking Time: 30 minutes

The List of Ingredients:

1. Salt and pepper as desired

2. 2 tablespoons butter

3. 1 tablespoon halal soy sauce

4. 4-5 spring onion, chopped

5. 2 eggs, whisked

6. 1 quart vegetable stock

Method:

Step 1	Put all ingredients (except eggs) in a deep-bottom pan.
Step 2	Use a lid to cover the pan. Let it simmer over the low heat until ingredients are cooked through and water reduces to half.
Step 3	Once ready, drizzle over eggs slowly over the soup while stirring continuously and cook until eggs are set
Step 4	Once ready, pour the soup into 2 bowls.
Step 5	Serve hot!

Recipe 23. Turnip Pumpkin Soup

Serves: 2

Preparation Time: 10 minutes

Cooking Time: 30 minutes

The List of Ingredients:

1. Salt and pepper to taste
2. 1/2 pound pumpkin, chopped
3. 1 quart vegetable stock
4. 2 cups turnip, chopped

5. 1 tablespoon freshly grated garlic

6. 2 tablespoons butter

Method:

Step 1   Put all the ingredients in a deep bottom pan.

Step 2   Cover the pan with a lid. Let it simmer over low heat until ingredients are cooked through and water reduces to half.

Step 3   Once ready, remove the pan from heat and pour the soup into 2 bowls.

Step 4   Serve hot!

Recipe 24. Tofu Peri-Peri Soup

Serves: 2

Preparation Time: 10 minutes

Cooking Time: 30 minutes

The List of Ingredients:

1. 2 tablespoons peri-peri sauce
2. 2 tablespoons butter
3. 1/2 pound firm tofu, diced
4. 1 quart vegetable stock

5. Salt and pepper to taste

Method:

Step 1   Put all the ingredients in a deep bottom pan.

Step 2   Cover the pan with a lid. Let it simmer over low heat until the water reduces to half.

Step 3   Once ready, remove the pan from heat and pour the soup into 2 bowls.

Step 4   Serve hot!

Recipe 25. Turnip Mutton Shorba

Serves: 2

Preparation Time: 10 minutes

Cooking Time: 30 minutes

The List of Ingredients:

1. Salt and pepper to taste

2. 1 quart halal chicken stock

3. 2-3 cardamoms, ground

4. 2 tablespoons butter

5. 2 cups turnip, chopped

6. 1/2 pound halal goat chunks, boneless

Method:

Step 1   Put all the ingredients in a deep bottom pan.

Step 2   Cover the pan with a lid. Let it simmer over low heat until ingredients are cooked through and water reduces to half.

Step 3   Once ready, remove the pan from heat and pour the soup into 2 bowls.

Step 4   Serve hot!

Recipe 26. Chicken Shorba

Serves: 2

Preparation Time: 10 minutes

Cooking Time: 30 minutes

The List of Ingredients:

1. 1 quart halal chicken stock
2. 2 tablespoons butter
3. Salt and pepper to taste
4. 1/2 cup sour cream

5. 2-3 star anise, crushed

6. 1/2 pound halal chicken breast, boneless

7. 2 tablespoons freshly grated ginger

Method:

Step 1 Put all the ingredients in a deep bottom pan.

Step 2 Cover the pan with a lid. Let it simmer over low heat until chicken is cooked through and water reduces to half.

Step 3 Once cooked, remove the lid and take out a chicken breast from the soup. Shred the chicken with a fork and put it back in the pan with soup. Cook for another 5 minutes over high heat, stirring occasionally.

Step 4 Once ready, remove the pan from heat and pour the soup into 2 bowls.

Step 5 Serve hot!

Recipe 27. Tomato Cream Soup

Serves: 2

Preparation Time: 10 minutes

Cooking Time: 30 minutes

The List of Ingredients:

1. 1 cup sour cream

2. 3 cups freshly pureed tomatoes

3. 2 tablespoons butter

4. 1 quart vegetable stock

5. Salt and pepper to taste

Method:

Step 1   Put all the ingredients in a deep bottom pan.

Step 2   Cover the pan with a lid. Let it simmer over low heat until the water reduces to half.

Step 3   Once ready, remove the pan from heat and pour the soup into 2 bowls.

Step 4   Serve hot!

Recipe 28. Cauliflower Cilantro Soup

Serves: 2

Preparation Time: 10 minutes

Cooking Time: 30 minutes

The List of Ingredients:

1. Juice of 1 lemon
2. 2 tablespoons butter
3. Florets of 1 medium head of cauliflower
4. Salt and pepper to taste

5. 1 quart vegetable stock

6. 2 cups fresh cilantro leaves

Method:

Step 1   Put all the ingredients in a deep bottom pan.

Step 2   Cover the pan with a lid. Let it simmer over low heat until ingredients are cooked through and water reduces to half.

Step 3   Once ready, remove the pan from heat and pour the soup into 2 bowls.

Step 4   Serve hot!

Recipe 29. Lentil French Bean Soup

Serves: 2

Preparation Time: 10 minutes

Cooking Time: 30 minutes

The List of Ingredients:

1. 1 quart vegetable stock
2. 1 tablespoon dried basil
3. 2 cups boiled lentils
4. Salt and pepper to taste

5. 2 tablespoons butter

6. 1/2 pound French beans, chopped

Method:

Step 1   Put all the ingredients in a deep bottom pan.

Step 2   Cover the pan with a lid. Let it simmer over low
           heat until ingredients are cooked through and
           water reduces to half.

Step 3   Once ready, remove the pan from heat and pour
           the soup into 2 bowls.

Step 4   Serve hot!

Salads

Recipe 30. Sweet Potato Honey Lemon Salad

Serves: 2

Preparation Time: 10 minutes

Cooking Time: 0 minutes

The List of Ingredients:

1. 1 tablespoon honey

2. Juice of 2 lemons

3. 1/2 pound boiled sweet potato, peeled and diced

4. Pepper to taste

Method:

Step 1   Combine all the ingredients in a large bowl and
           mix well.
Step 2   Serve!

Recipe 31. Apple Bread Salad

Serves: 2

Preparation Time: 10 minutes

Cooking Time: 0 minutes

The List of Ingredients:

1. Pepper to taste

2. 2 cups toasted bread, chopped

3. 1 small head of lettuce

4. 1/2 cup pureed avocado

5. 1 small white onion, chopped

6. 2 medium apples, chopped

Method:

Step 1   Combine all the ingredients in a large bowl and
          mix well.

Step 2   Serve!

Recipe 32. Corn Pear Salad

Serves: 2

Preparation Time: 10 minutes

Cooking Time: 0 minutes

The List of Ingredients:

1. 1 cup sweet corn kernels

2. 1 small head of lettuce

3. 2 tablespoons cream cheese

4. 2 medium pears, chopped

5. Pepper to taste

Method:

Step 1   Combine all the ingredients in a large bowl and
          mix well.
Step 2   Serve!

Recipe 33. Tofu Turnip Salad

Serves: 2

Preparation Time: 10 minutes

Cooking Time: 0 minutes

The List of Ingredients:

1. 1/4 pound halal firm tofu, diced

2. Pepper to taste

3. 2 teaspoons halal soy sauce

4. 1 small head of lettuce

5. 2 cups turnips, chopped

6. 1 small white onion, chopped

Method:

Step 1   Combine all the ingredients in a large bowl and
          mix well.

Step 2   Serve!

Recipe 34. Cabbage Cream Salad

Serves: 2

Preparation Time: 10 minutes

Cooking Time: 0 minutes

The List of Ingredients:

1. 1 small head of red cabbage, chopped

2. Pepper to taste

3. 1 small white onion, chopped

4. 1 small head of lettuce

5. 1/2 cup sour cream

6. 1 tablespoon halal vinegar

Method:

Step 1   Combine all the ingredients in a large bowl and
           mix well.
Step 2   Serve!

Recipe 35. Chicken Grape Salad

Serves: 2

Preparation Time: 10 minutes

Cooking Time: 0 minutes

The List of Ingredients:

1. 1/4 pound halal roasted chicken, shredded
2. 1 small head of lettuce
3. 2 cups black grapes
4. Pepper to taste

5. 1 small white onion, chopped

6. 1 teaspoon extra virgin olive oil

Method:

Step 1   Combine all the ingredients in a large bowl and mix well.

Step 2   Serve!

Recipe 36. Peanut Mustard Green Salad

Serves: 2

Preparation Time: 10 minutes

Cooking Time: 0 minutes

The List of Ingredients:

1. Pepper to taste

2. 1 cup roasted peanuts

3. 1 small head of lettuce

4. 1/4 pound mustard greens, chopped

5. 2 teaspoons peanut oil

6. 1 small white onion, chopped

84

Method:

Step 1   Combine all the ingredients in a large bowl and mix well.

Step 2   Serve!

Recipe 37. Parsley Pumpkin Salad

Serves: 2

Preparation Time: 10 minutes

Cooking Time: 0 minutes

The List of Ingredients:

1. 1 small head of lettuce
2. 2 fresh parsley leaves
3. Pepper to taste
4. 1/4 pound roasted pumpkin, diced

5. 2 teaspoons sesame oil

6. 1 small white onion, chopped

Method:

Step 1   Combine all the ingredients in a large bowl and mix well.

Step 2   Serve!

Recipe 38. Chicory Coriander Salad

Serves: 2

Preparation Time: 10 minutes

Cooking Time: 0 minutes

The List of Ingredients:

1. 1/4 chicory, chopped

2. Pepper to taste

3. 1 tablespoon halal French dressing

4. 1 small white onion, chopped

5. 2 cups fresh coriander leaves

6. 1 small head of lettuce

Method:

Step 1   Combine all the ingredients in a large bowl and mix well.

Step 2   Serve!

Recipe 39. Cucumber Carrot Salad

Serves: 2

Preparation Time: 10 minutes

Cooking Time: 0 minutes

The List of Ingredients:

1. 1 small white onion, chopped
2. Pepper to taste
3. 2 cups cucumbers, chopped
4. 2 cups carrots, julienne

5. 1 tablespoon halal mint sauce

6. 1 small head of lettuce

Method:

Step 1 Combine all the ingredients in a large bowl and mix well.

Step 2 Serve!

Recipe 40. Salmon Broccoli Salad

Serves: 2

Preparation Time: 10 minutes

Cooking Time: 0 minutes

The List of Ingredients:

1. 1/4 pound halal butter-fried salmon, shredded

2. 1 small white onion, chopped

3. Pepper to taste

4. 1/2 cup mozzarella cheese

5. 1 small head of lettuce

6. florets of 1 head of broccoli

Method:

Step 1   Combine all the ingredients in a large bowl and mix well.

Step 2   Serve!

Recipe 41. Bean Cherry Tomato Salad

Serves: 2

Preparation Time: 10 minutes

Cooking Time: 0 minutes

The List of Ingredients:

1. 1 small head of lettuce

2. Pepper to taste

3. 2 cups cherry tomatoes, halved

4. 1 small white onion, chopped

5. 1/4 pound boiled red kidney beans

6. 2 tablespoons tahini

Method:

Step 1   Combine all the ingredients in a large bowl and
          mix well.

Step 2   Serve!

Recipe 42. Spinach Potato Salad

Serves: 2

Preparation Time: 10 minutes

Cooking Time: 0 minutes

The List of Ingredients:

1. Pepper to taste
2. 1/4 pound baby spinach leaves
3. 1 small white onion, chopped
4. 1/2 cup fresh hummus

5. 2 medium boiled potatoes, diced

6. 1 small head of lettuce

Method:

Step 1   Combine all the ingredients in a large bowl and
           mix well.

Step 2   Serve!

Recipe 43. Beef Sesame Salad

Serves: 2

Preparation Time: 10 minutes

Cooking Time: 0 minutes

The List of Ingredients:

1. 1 small head of lettuce

2. 1 small white onion, chopped

3. 1/4 pound butter-fried halal beef, minced

4. Pepper to taste

5. 2 tablespoons halal mayo

6. 1/2 cup roasted sesame seeds

Method:

Step 1   Combine all the ingredients in a large bowl and
           mix well.

Step 2   Serve!

Recipe 44. Egg Salad

Serves: 2

Preparation Time: 10 minutes

Cooking Time: 0 minutes

The List of Ingredients:

1. Pepper to taste
2. 1/4 pound halal roasted chicken, shredded

3.   1 small white onion, chopped

4.   1 small head of lettuce

5.   1 teaspoon extra virgin olive oil

6.   2 cups black grapes

Method:

Step 1   Combine all the ingredients in a large bowl and
           mix well.

Step 2   Serve!

Smoothies

Recipe 45. Pineapple Banana Smoothie

Serves: 2

Preparation Time: 10 minutes

Cooking Time: 0 minutes

The List of Ingredients:

1. 2 cups pineapple, chopped
2. 2 medium bananas, chopped

Method:

Step 1   Blend all the ingredients in a food processor until smooth and pour the prepared smoothie into two glasses.

Step 2   Serve!

Recipe 46. Strawberry Apple Smoothie

Serves: 2

Preparation Time: 10 minutes

Cooking Time: 0 minutes

The List of Ingredients:

1. 2 cups strawberries, hulled
2. 1 medium banana, chopped
3. 2 cups apple, chopped

Method:

Step 1   Blend all the ingredients in a food processor until smooth and pour the prepared smoothie into two glasses.

Step 2   Serve!

Recipe 47. Pomegranate Cherry Smoothie

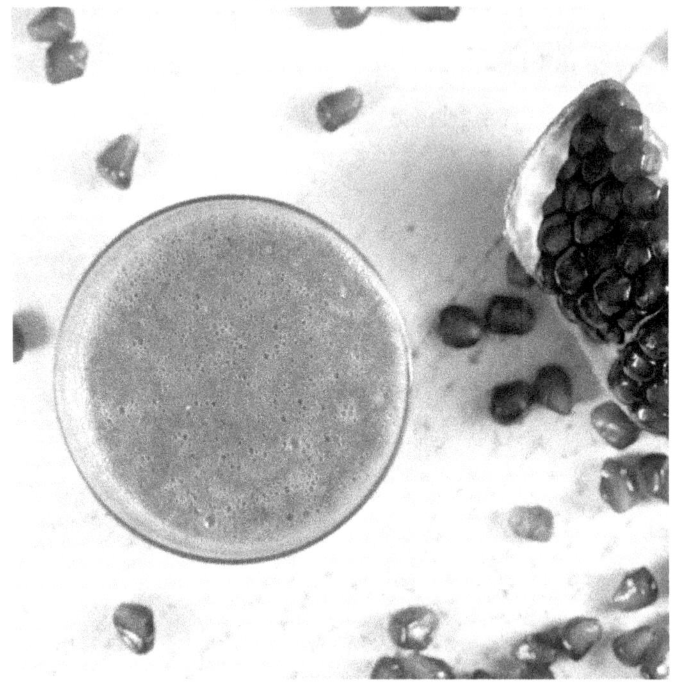

Serves: 2

Preparation Time: 10 minutes

Cooking Time: 0 minutes

The List of Ingredients:

1. 2 cups cherries, deseeded

2. 2 cups pomegranate kernels

3. 1 medium banana, chopped

Method:

Step 1   Blend all the ingredients in a food processor
          until smooth and pour the prepared smoothie
          into two glasses.
Step 2   Serve!

Recipe 48. Pear Peach Smoothie

Serves: 2

Preparation Time: 10 minutes

Cooking Time: 0 minutes

The List of Ingredients:

1. 2 cups pears, chopped
2. 1 medium banana, chopped
3. 2 cups peaches, chopped

Method:

Step 1   Blend all the ingredients in a food processor
          until smooth and pour the prepared smoothie
          into two glasses.

Step 2   Serve!

Recipe 49. Grape Kiwi Smoothie

Serves: 2

Preparation Time: 10 minutes

Cooking Time: 0 minutes

The List of Ingredients:

1. 2 cups grapes

2. 1 medium banana, chopped

3. 2 cups kiwi fruit, chopped

Method:

Step 1   Blend all the ingredients in a food processor until smooth and pour the prepared smoothie into two glasses.

Step 2   Serve!

www.ingramcontent.com/pod-product-compliance
Lightning Source LLC
Chambersburg PA
CBHW071536150726

48000CB00002B/821